Acrylics

MASTERCLASS

hinkler

Contents

Published by Hinkler Pty Ltd 2018
45–55 Fairchild Street
Heatherton Victoria 3202 Australia
www.hinkler.com

hinkler
Text © Anness Publishing Ltd

Painting, Photography and Illustration © Anness Publishing Ltd 2014, except for the painting on pg. 48
that is © Laurin Rinder/Shutterstock.com and the illustrations of artistic tools © Shutterstock.com

Cover design: Sam Grimmer
Author: Ian Sidaway
Internal design: Tanya Bickers and Patricia Hodges
Prepress: Splitting Image

ISBN: 978 1 4889 3862 7

Printed and bound in China

Introduction

Perhaps the most important and far-reaching advance in artists' materials in the last 100 years has been the formulation of water-mixable acrylic paint. Acrylic resins were formulated in the 1920s and 1930s, although it took several years before a liquid acrylic emulsion that dried to a clear film was used to carry and bind together pigment. The first commercially available paint based on these emulsions was made available in the 1950s.

Acrylic paint can be mixed with a wide range of acrylic mediums and additives and is thinned with water. Unlike oil paint, it dries quickly and the paint film remains extremely flexible and will not crack. The paint can be used with a wide range of techniques, from thick layers, to thin, semi-transparent washes, as with watercolour. Indeed, most if not all of the techniques used in both oil and watercolour painting can be used with acrylic paint. Acrylic paint should not be thought of as an alternative to either, however, but as a very adaptable and unique painting material in its own right.

Acrylic paint is made by suspending pigment in an acrylic emulsion; in some paint formulations, several slightly different emulsions are combined. The paint may also contain various dispersants to ensure the uniform distribution of the pigments, plus defoamers, preservatives and thickeners.

Both students' and artists' quality acrylic paint is available. Artists' quality paint is available in a wide range of colours, with the cost depending on the pigments used. A less extensive range of colours is available in the students' range and the cost is the same across the whole range.

Acrylic paints come in three different consistencies. Tube paint tends to be of a buttery consistency and holds its shape when squeezed from the tube. Tub paint is thinner and more creamy in consistency, which makes it easier to brush out and cover large areas. There are also liquid acrylic colours that are the consistency of ink and are often sold as acrylic inks.

Characteristics of acrylic paint

The pigments in acrylic paints are bound with an acrylic resin that is water soluble and virtually odour free. Because it is water soluble, the paint is very easy to use, requiring only the addition of clean water. Water is also all that is needed to clean up wet paint after a work session. Once it has dried, however, acrylic paint creates a permanent hard-but-flexible film that will not fade or crack and is impervious to further applications of acrylic or oil paint and any of their associated mediums or solvents. Acrylic paint dries relatively quickly: a thin film will be touch dry in a few minutes and even thicker applications dry in a matter of hours.

Texture gels
Various gels can be mixed into acrylic paint to give a range of textural effects. These can be worked into while the paint is still wet.

Mediums and additives
A wide range of mediums and additives can be mixed into acrylic paint to alter and enhance its handling characteristics.

Adhesive qualities
Many acrylic mediums have very good adhesive qualities, making them ideal for collage work.

All acrylic colours, depending on the thickness of paint used, dry at the same rate.

Although hardened paint can be removed with strong paint strippers, this will quickly ruin your brushes. Wet paint, however, can easily be removed by rinsing the brush in water. Try to get into the habit of rinsing your brushes regularly as you work.

Paint can also quickly dry on the palette, although you can avoid this by laying out and mixing only small quantities of paint and by spraying your palette periodically with clean water or using a special 'stay-wet' palette.

The unique qualities of acrylic paint mean that many of the techniques that are commonly used with both oil paint and watercolour can be used. Acrylic paint is excellent when used for underpainting prior to completing a work in oils, but it should not be used over oil paint.

Thinned with water and used on paper, acrylic paint behaves like watercolour paint – the big difference being that once it is dry, acrylic paint is no longer re-soluble. It also behaves like oil paint and can be used thickly, straight from the tube, to build up heavily textured areas of paint. Unlike oil paint though, it dries in a matter of minutes – and this can make blending colours together, even over a small area, somewhat difficult.

Extending drying time
The drying time of acrylic paint can be extended by using a retarding medium, which gives you longer to work into the paint and blend colours.

Glazing with acrylics
Acrylic colours can be glazed by thinning the paint with water, although a better result is achieved by adding an acrylic medium.

Covering power
Acrylic paint applied straight from the tube has good covering power, even when applying a light colour over a dark one.

Shape-holding ability
Acrylic paint that is applied thickly, straight from the tube, holds its shape and the mark of the brush as it dries.

Colours

Mixing colours

You only technically need three paint colours to make all the other colours of the rainbow: the primary colours (red, blue and yellow).

Primary colours are mixed to create the 'secondary colours' orange, violet and green:

red + yellow = orange
blue + yellow = green
blue + red = violet

Tertiary colours are formed by mixing equal amounts (50% each) of a primary and secondary colour.

These include the following common combinations:

red + white = pink
red + green = brown

Technically they fall into these six categories:

● red-orange

● yellow-orange

● yellow-green

● blue-green

● blue-violet

● red–violet

Choosing colours

To avoid complex and laborious mixing, however, it is useful to have a good range of colours when you start on your artistic journey of acrylic painting. Having at least one shade of each primary colour and one of each of the secondary colours is ideal.

Alternatively, another great starting point is to have both warm and cool versions of the three primary colours (so two reds, two blues and two yellows), as well as a green colour, a violet colour, at least one earthy-toned colour, and a white and a black or neutral grey.

Here's a suggestion of colours you might choose to begin with:

● A 'warm' blue, for instance *ultramarine blue*

● A 'cool' blue, for instance, *cerulean blue*

● A 'warm' red, for instance *cadmium red*

● A 'cool' red, for instance *Alizarin crimson*

● A 'bright' yellow, for instance *lemon yellow*

● An 'earthy' yellow, for instance *yellow ochre*

● An 'earthy' brown, for instance *raw umber*

● A 'warm' brown, for instance *burnt sienna*

● A 'bright' green, for instance *grass green*

● A black, for instance *ivory black*

● A white, for instance *titanium white*

For the exercises and examples in this book, we identify the specific colours used, along with any colour mixes; however, you don't need to match these exactly. If you prefer, you can even substitute completely different colours if you want to. Just read the exercise through to see what impact (if any) a change of colour might have on your ability to practice the skill or technique being explored. As you become more experienced and skilful, you may decide to invest in a larger range of colours, but to begin with, a basic palette and substituted or approximated colours are fine.

Palettes

The surface on which an artist arranges colours prior to mixing them and applying them to the support is known as the palette. Somewhat confusingly, the same word is also used to describe the range of colours used by a particular artist, or the range of colours found in a particular painting.

Plastic palettes

Wooden palettes are not recommended for acrylic paint, as the hardened paint can be difficult to remove. White plastic palettes, by contrast, have an impervious surface, which makes them ideal for use with acrylic paint. They are easy to clean, although the surface can become stained after using very strong colours such as viridian or phthalocyanine blue.

Stay-wet palettes

A stay-wet palette will help prevent acrylic paints from drying out and becoming unworkable too quickly. These palettes have a shallow, recessed tray into which a water-impregnated membrane is placed. The paint is placed and mixed on this membrane.

If you want to leave a painting halfway through and come back to it later, you can place a plastic cover over the tray, sealing the moist paint in the palette. Store the palette in a cool place, or even in the refrigerator. If the membrane dries out, you can simply re-wet it.

Paintbrushes

Brushes are available in a wide range of shapes and sizes, from tiny brushes that consist of just a few hairs or fibres that are used to paint very fine detail to large, flat brushes several centimetres (inches) across. Most brushes are sold in series, with each brush being given a number depending on its size: the higher the number, the larger the brush.

The cost of a brush depends on the quality of the materials from which it is made and on its size. Good-quality brushes are worth their initial high cost as, provided you look after them, they will last longer than cheaper alternatives.

Brush materials

The materials used to make brush fibres may be either natural or synthetic, hard or soft.

Bristle brushes are traditionally made from hog hair. The bristles hold their shape well and the fibres are thick, which means they can hold a substantial amount of paint. In the very best bristle brushes, the end of each bristle is split; this is known as 'flagging', and it allows the bristle to hold more paint and distribute it evenly.

Synthetic brushes are good quality and hard wearing. They are also less expensive than either bristle or natural-hair brushes. However, they can quickly lose their shape if they are not looked after and cleaned well.

Natural hair brushes can be made from sable, goat, squirrel, ox and even mongoose hair. Traditionally, natural hair brushes are more often associated with watercolour painting, but they can also be used with acrylics; as painting in acrylics draws on techniques that are used in both watercolour and oil painting.

Cleaning brushes

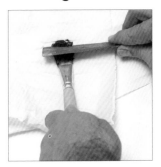

1. Cleaning your brushes thoroughly will make them last longer. Wipe off excess paint on a rag or a piece of scrap paper, then scrape off as much paint as you can using a palette knife.

2. Pour a small amount of water into a jar; you will need enough to cover the bristles of the brush. Agitate the brush in the jar, pressing it against the sides to dislodge any dried-on paint.

3. Rub detergent into the bristles, then rinse the brush thoroughly in clean water. Reshape the bristles with your fingertips and store the brush with the bristles pointing upwards, so they hold their shape.

Brush shapes

Several brush shapes are available in synthetic fibres and natural hair. Although the choice might seem bewildering at first glance, some of the more 'specialist' brushes are of limited use, and you would probably do better to experiment with a small range and find out what kind of marks you can make with each one.

Do not overlook the range of brushes available from home improvement stores: decorators' brushes can be very useful for laying in large areas of colour – when toning a ground, for example. These are often of a very high quality and cost far less than similar brushes sold in art supply stores.

- -

Brushes for fine detail

A rigger brush (to the far left below) is very long and thin. It was originally invented for painting the straight lines of the ropes and rigging on ships in marine painting – hence the rather odd-sounding name.
A liner (second left) is a flat brush which has the end cut away at an angle. Both of these brushes may be made from natural or synthetic fibres.

Wash brushes

The wash brush has a wide body, which holds a large quantity of paint. It is used for covering largeareas with a uniform or flat wash of paint. Flat wash brushes (third left) are best suited to use with acrylics.

Flat brushes

These brushes have square ends. They hold a lot of paint, which can be applied as short impasto strokes or brushed out flat. Large flat brushes are useful for blocking in and covering large areas quickly. Short flats, known as 'brights', hold less paint and are stiffer. They make precise, short strokes, ideal for detail and texture work.

Round brushes

These are round-headed brushes that are used for detail and for single-stroke marks. Larger round brushes hold a lot of paint and are useful for the initial blocking-in. The point on a round brush can be quickly worn down by rough surfaces. The brushes shown here are made of natural hair.

Unusually shaped brushes

Fan blenders (second right) are intended for blending together colours. They are also useful for special effects such as drybrush work. A filbert (far right) combines some of the qualities of a flat and a round brush.

Rigger brush
Liner brush
Flat wash brush
Large flat brush
Short flat brush
Small round brush
Large round brush
Fan bender brush
Filbert

Using different brushes

Here are some examples of the kind of marks you can make with round and flat brush shapes. It's well worth practising these marks with the brushes you purchase, to get a feel for each one applies paint.

Round brushes

Short strokes
With the brush handle more or less parallel to the support (see page 11), you can quickly build up an area of paint with short strokes.

Rounded marks
Holding the brush at 45 degrees to the support means that you are using the tip of the brush. This creates more rounded marks.

Dots
Holding the brush almost perpendicular to the support and dabbing it on to the support creates small dots and stipples.

Long strokes
Stroking the brush over the support as if you were drawing with a pencil allows you to make long, flowing marks.

Flat brushes

Long strokes
Making long strokes with a flat brush held parallel to the support, the wedge-like shape of the brush head is evident.

Short strokes
Short, wedge-shaped strokes can be used to deliver thick paint to the support – a technique used to create heavy texture.

Dots
Holding the brush almost perpendicular to the support and dabbing it on creates short lines and wedge-shaped marks.

Thin strokes
Use the edge of the brush to make thin marks (straight or curved), applying light pressure so as not to splay the bristles.

Rough, uneven texture
Scrubbing on paint using the side of the brush creates a rough, uneven texture that is ideal when you want to cover a large area but do not want a flat wash of colour.

Rough, uneven texture
Scrubbing on paint using the side of the brush creates a rough, uneven texture in the same way as with a round brush and is useful for scumbling one colour over another.

Other means of applying paint

Brushes are the obvious means of applying paint, but there are also many other things that you can use to make marks. Some are designed specifically for painting, while others are everyday household items. Experiment to see what effects you can achieve. Dip fabrics, from coarse but evenly textured linen to pretty, delicate lace, into paint to transfer their patterns to the support; press twigs, pieces of cardboard, or even out-of-date credit cards into paint and scrape them over your painting surface to make straight lines; dip scrunched-up aluminium foil or plastic food wrap in paint and press it on to the support to make random textures; even apply paint with your fingers.

Unusual paint applicators

There is a huge range of ready-made paint applicators on the market – some of which are useful, while others are little more than manufacturers' gimmicks. Each type makes a different kind of mark.

Paint shaper

Available in a range of sizes and forms, paint shapers consist of a shaped rubber tip fitted into a metal ferrule, which in turn is fitted into a wooden handle, just like a brush. The type of mark you can make depends on the size and shape of the tip.

Foam roller

Foam paint-rollers are a great way of covering a large area quickly, and can also be used to achieve textural effects. They are available in various sizes and are inexpensive enough to be discarded when they become too dirty to use.

Foam brush

This consists of a wedge of synthetic foam attached to a handle. It can be dragged across the support to make broad marks in which the texture of the foam is evident. You can also dip the tip in the paint to make straight lines.

Sponge

Sponges are a great way of creating texture for things like lichen on stone or random clouds and are particularly useful for landscape work. Synthetic sponges give a more even texture than the natural sponge shown here.

Rag or paper

Rags and scrunched-up absorbent paper are used in the same way as sponges to create textured marks for particular subjects, although the textures that they create tend to be more irregular.

Supports

A 'support' is the name for the surface on which a painting is made. It needs to be physically stable and resistant to deterioration from both the corrosive nature of any of the materials being used and the surrounding atmosphere. It needs to be light enough to be transported from one place to another. It also needs to have a sympathetic surface texture, as this will have a direct effect on the marks and techniques that you use.

Canvas

Without doubt, canvas is the most widely used support for acrylic work. Several types of canvas are available, made from different fibres. The most common are made from either cotton or linen, both of which can be purchased ready-stretched and primed to a range of standard sizes (although there are suppliers who will prepare supports to any size) or on the roll by the metre (yard) either primed or unprimed. Unprimed canvas is easier to stretch.

Linen canvas is made from the fibres of the flax plant, *Linum usitatissimum*. The seeds of this plant are also pressed to make linseed oil, used by artists. Linen is the finest type of canvas available. It is light brown in colour, very strong, and provides a pleasingly receptive surface on which to work. Depending on the gauge or weight of the thread used, linen canvas can have a wide variety of weave textures and weights. It is often described as being fine, medium or coarse. As a general rule, lighter weights (200-225 g/7-8 oz) with a fine tooth are used for smaller works, while heavier grades (375-450 g/12-15 oz) are best for larger works. Because of the way linen is woven, the surface texture never looks too even or mechanical.

Cotton canvas is known as cotton duck. It is light cream in colour and has a more regular or mechanical weave than linen. Stretched cotton duck is more stable than linen and is less prone to becoming slack on its stretcher if the air becomes damp. Seen as inferior to linen, it is nonetheless a popular and widely used support. It is substantially cheaper than linen and is also easier to stretch. Cotton duck is available in a range of weights from 200-450 g/7-15 oz; for larger works, use weights over 250 g/10 oz.

Linen canvas ▶

Cotton duck ▼

Stretching canvas

Canvas must be stretched taut over a rectangular wooden frame, made up of stretcher bars that are slotted together. The cross bars should be able to support canvas sizes of 75 x 100 cm/30 x 40 in or more).

The wooden wedges are tapped lightly into each corner and allow you to increase the tension of the stretched canvas a little if necessary.

1 Press or tap the stretcher bars together to make a frame. They should slot together easily, without you having to exert much pressure.

2 Using a tape measure or piece of string, measure diagonally from corner to corner in both directions to check that the corners are square.

3 Lay the canvas flat and place the frame on top, bevelled side down. Cut out, allowing an overlap of approximately the width of the stretcher bars on all sides.

4 Fold the excess canvas over the stretcher bars, ensuring the threads run parallel to the bars, and staple into the centre of opposite sides. Repeat on the other sides.

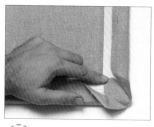

5 Add two more staples to each bar, either side of the centre staple and evenly spaced. Then, fold in one canvas corner and hold it in position.

6 Fold over the flap of canvas on one side of the corner, pull it taut and hold it firmly in position with your fingertip.

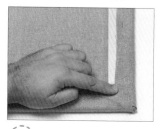

7 Fold over the remaining flap of canvas and secure with a staple, keeping your finger well away from the staple gun.

8 In each corner, push two wedges into the slots in the stretcher bars. If the canvas sags, the wedges can be pushed in further to keep the canvas taut.

Boards

Several types of wooden board make good supports for acrylic work. The boards can simply be primed with an acrylic gesso, or canvas can be glued to the surface; a technique known as marouflaging. There are three types of board in common use: plywood, hardboard (masonite) and medium-density fibreboard (MDF).

Plywood is made from several thin layers of wood or veneers glued together to form a rigid sheet. The surface veneers are usually made from hardwood and are smooth.

Hardboard is made from exploded wood fibre and is available both tempered and untempered. Tempering with oils or resins makes it harder and more water resistant. Use the softer-surfaced, untempered board, as the hard and somewhat oily surface of tempered board can resist paint. Some hardboards have a rough and a smooth side; you can paint on either side, depending on the effect you want.

MDF, made from compacted wood fibres, is perhaps the best board to use as it is stable and warp resistant. Both sides of MDF are hard and smooth.

All these boards can be found in a range of sizes. If used at a size where they begin to bend, mount rigid wooden battens on the reverse side to reinforce them.

Priming board

Wood was traditionally sized with rabbit-skin glue and then primed with a thixotropic primer in the same way as canvas; nowadays, most artists use ready-made acrylic primer or acrylic gesso primer, which excludes the need for sizing. Acrylic primer also dries much more quickly.

Before you prime your boards, make sure they are smooth and free of dust. You should also wipe over them with methylated spirits to remove all traces of grease.

1 Using a wide, flat brush or a decorator's brush, apply primer over the board with smooth, vertical strokes. For a very large surface, apply the primer with a paint roller. Allow to dry.

2 Rub the surface of the board with fine-grade sandpaper to smooth out any ridges in the paint. Blow or dust off any powder.

3 Apply another coat of primer, making smooth horizontal strokes. Allow to dry. Repeat as many times as you wish, sanding between coats.

Covering board with canvas

Canvas-covered board is a lightweight painting surface that is particularly useful when you are painting on location. It combines the strength and low cost of board with the texture of canvas. You can use linen or cotton duck, which makes it a good way of using up remnants of canvas; calico, which is a cheap material, is also suitable. Acrylic primer is used to stick the canvas to the board. It looks white when it is first applied, but dries clear. When you have stuck the canvas on to the board, you should leave it to dry for an hour or two in a warm room. Prime the canvas with an acrylic primer before use.

1 Arrange the canvas on a flat surface. Place the board on the canvas. Allowing a 5cm/2in overlap all around, cut out the canvas with a pair of sharp scissors.

2 Remove the canvas from the work surface. Using a wide, flat brush or a household decorator's brush, liberally brush matt acrylic medium over the surface of the board.

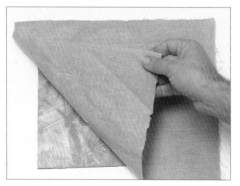

3 Place the canvas on the sticky side of the board and smooth it out with your fingertips, working from the centre outwards.

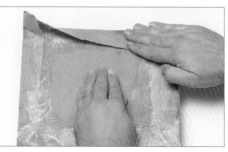

4 Brush acrylic medium over the canvas to make sure that it is firmly stuck down. Place the board canvas-side down on an upturned plate so that it does not stick to your work surface. Brush medium on the edges of the board. Fold over the excess canvas, along all sides and fold the corners so that they make a 90° angle. Then stick it all down with acrylic medium.

Canvas paper and board

Artists' canvas boards are made by laminating canvas – or paper textured to look like canvas – on to cardboard. They are made in several sizes and textures and are ideal for use when painting on location. However, take care not to get them wet, as the cardboard backing will disintegrate. They can also be easily damaged if you drop them on their corners. They come in a variety of sizes.

Oil and acrylic papers are also available (you can use oil papers for acrylic, but acrylic papers are better). Both have a texture similar to canvas and can be bought as loose sheets or as sheets bound together in blocks. Although they are perhaps not suitable for work that is intended to last, they are perfect for sketching and making colour notes.

Oil and acrylic papers

Acrylic additives

There are a wide range of mediums and additives that accentuate or modify aspects of acrylic paints as a medium. Scour the shelves of any good art supply store and you will find additives that make the paint finish gloss or matt, thick or thin, textured or smooth. There are additives that slow down the drying time of the paint, giving you longer to work into it. There are even additives that make colours glow in the dark or turn acrylic into a fabric paint that can withstand being put through a washing machine. The chances are that if you want to do something creative with acrylic paint, there is an additive to enable you to do it.

Varnishes

Varnish is applied to paintings to protect them from atmospheric pollution and dirt. A varnish also unifies and enhances the colour, bringing the whole painted surface together beneath a uniform gloss or semi-matt sheen.

A painting must be completely dry before it is varnished, otherwise the drying paint will contract beneath the less flexible varnish and cause it to crack. Acrylic paintings can be safely varnished after a few hours.

Applying varnish
Always work in a dust-free environment. Place your dry painting flat. Dip a large, clean, flat brush in your chosen acrylic varnish and apply it in smooth, even strokes in one direction. Do not scrub the surface or you will create air bubbles. If you go over any area more than once, the finish will be uneven.

Tone

If you want to show that an object is three-dimensional, you need to master the art of depicting tone. Used well, tone can also play an important part in conveying mood and atmosphere. Tone is simply the relative lightness or darkness of a colour. Another term that you may come across in art books is 'value' – but the meaning is exactly the same.

The apparent lightness or darkness of a subject depends on several things. First, it depends on the quality, intensity and direction of the light source: if one side of an object is brightly lit, it will be lighter in value than the side that is in shadow or shielded from the light. Second, the tone depends on the relative lightness or darkness of the colours present within that subject.

In order to create the illusion of three-dimensional form on a flat, two-dimensional surface, more than one tone needs to be in evidence. If you draw a circle and paint it a uniform mid-tone red, all you will see is a flat red disc. If, however, you paint one side of your circle red and then gradually darken that red colour as you paint across the circle to the other side, the circle appears to become a sphere, one side apparently hit by the light and the other side in shadow.

Colours and tonal equivalents

Although there are hundreds of tonal values between black and white, the brain can only distinguish the differences between a few – as shown in the tonal scale, above. The second row shows the tonal equivalent – the relative lightness or darkness – of a number of different hues.

In general, strong light makes colours appear brighter and more intense. It also increases the tonal gap: that is, the range of tones evident between the lightest tone and the darkest. This is known as contrast. An image with a strong tonal contrast will look more three-dimensional and appear to have greater depth than an image that lacks contrast.

Colour also has an important part to play when you are assessing tonal values. When you are painting an image, a black object in bright light still needs to look black, just as a white object in shadow still needs to look white. A light-coloured object in bright light or deep shadow will look lighter than a dark colour in light or shade. In reality, however, very different colours can have the same tonal value, with even comparatively light colours looking surprisingly dark in the right lighting conditions. Perhaps the best way to appreciate this is to look at a black-and-white photograph, where colours that are very different can look tonally the same or at least very similar.

Pure hues have distinct tonal values. Prussian blue is very dark in value, while lemon yellow is very light. This is best seen when positioning a hue against its matching tonal value on a value scale. However, similar hues can have very different tonal values, while different hues can be very similar in tone.

Lightening colours
To lighten a colour, add white paint.

Darkening colours
To darken a colour, add black paint.

Painting project: Seeing in tones

This exercise, painted in shades of grey, provides the opportunity to translate colours into tone. You may be surprised to discover that colours that you think of as being very different – the red of the capsicum and chillies and the green of the broccoli, for example – are very similar in tone. Note, too, how many variations in tone there are within one colour – for example, in the white areas of the cloths.

In this exercise, the very brightest areas are left unpainted. Start by working out where these are, and then where the next lightest tone occurs. Working from light to dark in this way allows you to build up the tones gradually. Remember that acrylic paint looks slightly darker when it is dry; you may wish to test your mixtures first on scrap paper. Also, be prepared to reassess matters once you've put down several tones, and make adjustments if necessary.

- -

The set-up

This still life contains all three primary colours – red, yellow and blue – as well as black and white. The tablecloths and the lemons may turn out to be darker than you might imagine, while even the darkest object (the eggplant) contains areas of bright highlight.

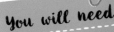

you will need

- B pencil
- Canvas board
- Acrylic paints: ebony black, titanium white
- Brushes: small flat

1 Using a B pencil, lightly sketch the subject. Put in as much detail as you need: although it's quite time-consuming to draw the checks of the cloths, for example, they will enable you to place the shifts in tone accurately. Similarly, the highlights on the vegetables will help you to define their form.

2 Mix the lightest tone from ebony black and titanium white. Using a small flat brush, paint the highlights on the eggplant, broccoli stalk, capsicums and cloths. Use the same tone for the garlic, lemons and the blade of the topmost knife, except for the very brightest highlights.

3. Look carefully to see where colours change tone. Add a little black to the mixture to darken it and paint the shadows on the plate, the shaded edges of the lemons and the broccoli florets. Go over the first tone where necessary to darken it.

4. Now add more black to the paint for your third tone. Darken the individual segments and the papery top of the garlic. Brush over the wooden table and chopping board, taking care to cut around any light areas.

5. The chopping board is darker than the table on which it rests, so add still more black to the paint to make tone 4 and go over the chopping board again. Use the same tone to deepen the shadows on the capsicums and chillies. Also use it to paint the rivets on the knife handles and the blade of the lower knife, which is somewhat tarnished and darker in tone.

Helpful Hint

You may find it helps to switch to a smaller brush, as you're working on very small, crisply defined areas at this stage in the painting.

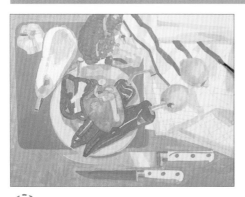

6. Darken any tones that now look too pale. Add more black to make tone 5, then dab the paint over the broccoli florets, leaving the underlying tone showing through in places. Use the same tone on the large red capsicum and chillies, leaving the highlights untouched, and on the blue-and-white cloth in the background.

7. Still using tone 5, continue working on the cloths. Note how the direction of the stripes changes with the folds in the cloth. Paint a thin shadow under the edge of the chopping board; this helps to separate it from the table. Paint the dark parts of the handle of the topmost knife.

8 Add more black to make tone 6 and paint the darkest parts of the blue-and-white cloth – the squares where two blue bands overlap. Paint the eggplant, brushing around the light areas, and the handle of the lower knife.

9 Using tone 6, darken the left-hand side of the red pepper. Add more black to make the darkest tone. Paint a thin strip along the top of the topmost knife. Use the same tone for the darkest parts of the eggplant and chillies.

The finished painting

In this painting, seven tones plus the white of the support have been used to portray a multi-coloured still life. When you've done this exercise, you might like to try setting up another multi-coloured still life. Although it might seem difficult at first, you will quickly become adept at interpreting colours as tones; it is a vital part of making your paintings look rounded and three-dimensional.

The pale green of the broccoli stalk is almost the same tone as the yellow capsicum, although you might expect it to be considerably darker.

The darkest part of the chilli is almost as dark as the eggplant, although you might expect it to be lighter in tone.

Don't assume that things you know to be white will actually appear pure white: as you can see, some tone is evident in the white of the cloth.

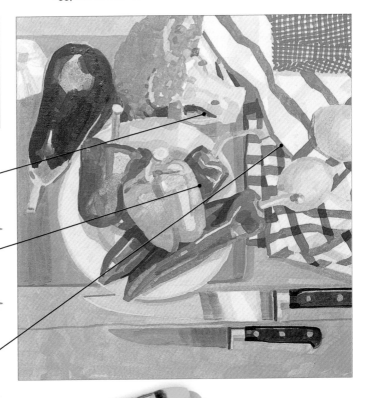

Scaling up

Whether you're painting from a photo or from life via a quick sketch, once you've got your reference material, how do you transfer it on to a larger canvas or support?

It takes a certain amount of confidence to do this purely by eye. Luckily, there is a tried-and-tested means of scaling up. It involves superimposing a grid on your preliminary sketch or photo and marking a larger grid on your canvas. You can then copy the scene, one square at a time, and the lines of the grid will give you a good guide to where to position things.

In a complicated scene, such as a building, you might want to subdivide some of the squares. Any method that enables you to keep track of where you are in the sketch is fine.

You can also scale up your photograph or sketch using a photocopier. This is helpful if you're not sure of your final size, as you can make several sizes to review.

If you have access to a scanner, you can also scan your image, enlarge it using photo-editing software and then print it out at the desired size. If your final size is too large for your printer you can try printing it out in sections.

Projectors are another easy way to scale up. Simply project the image onto your desired support at the correct size, then carefully trace over the projected image.

Acetate grid over photograph
Draw a grid on acetate (available from craft and art supply stores) and place it over your photograph. Then draw a grid on your paper or canvas, keeping the same proportions. If, for example, the grid on your photo is five squares across and four squares down, the grid on your canvas should be the same – although the squares will be larger. You can then transfer the contents of each square in turn to make your underdrawing or sketch.

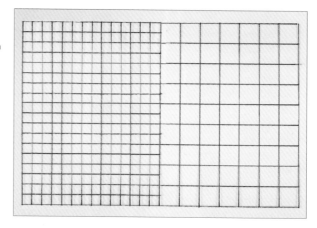

Different-sized squares within the same grid
In areas where you need more guidelines, simply divide the squares of the grid into smaller squares.

Painting Project: Scaling up a small sketch

Here's a more detailed breakdown of how to scale up a pencil sketch using the grid method. You can draw the grid directly on your sketch, if you wish, or use acetate as described opposite.

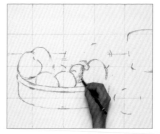

1 Divide up your sketch with a grid of evenly sized squares. The number of squares is up to you, but they should all be the same size.

2 Then lightly mark a grid on your canvas and lightly mark the main intersections – the points where the edges of your subject touch the grid lines.

3 Start joining up the intersections, working square by square and referring continually to your initial sketch.

4 Continue transferring information until your underdrawing is complete. If you wish, you can also put in some shading to act as a tonal guide.

The finished underdrawing

When you have put down as much information as you need, you can begin the process of painting. The amount of detail that you put into your underdrawing depends at least in part on the complexity of your subject and is entirely up to you. Remember that an underdrawing is merely a guide to help you place elements correctly and work out the tones.

Toned grounds

Some artists like to paint on a coloured, or toned, ground rather than on white canvas or paper. There are two main reasons for this. First, it can be difficult to assess colours and tones against a white ground, particularly in the early stages of a painting: it is much easier to start on a mid-toned ground.

Second, a toned ground establishes an overall colour 'key' or mood for your painting. If you allow the colour of the ground to show through in places, it helps to unify the painting.

A toned ground may be either transparent or opaque. On a transparent ground, some of the colour of the support is reflected back up through the paint, giving a more luminous, vibrant feel. For this method, the paint should be heavily diluted and spread in a thin layer. An opaque ground is used with opaque painting methods, such as impasto. For an opaque ground, mix your chosen colour with either white paint or primer.

What colour should you use to tone the ground? Some artists use a colour in keeping with the subject – earthy brown for a landscape, for example. Others prefer a contrast, such as a hint of yellow beneath a brilliant blue sky.

How to tone a ground

Whether you apply paint with a rag or with a brush is largely a matter of personal preference. The important thing is to use a thin layer of paint. It doesn't matter if some brush strokes are visible or if the paint is slightly streaked; in fact, this gives a more lively, spontaneous effect.

Applying paint with a rag

1 Dab your chosen colour over the canvas.

2 Dip a rag in water and rub it over the canvas to spread the paint. It is a good idea to wear rubber gloves. Leave to dry.

The prepared ground

Applying paint with a brush

1 Mix a thin wash of your chosen colour and, using a large, flat brush, apply the paint to the surface, varying the direction of the brushstrokes.

The prepared ground

Always allow the prepared, toned ground to dry completely before you begin your painting.

Helpful Hint

Whatever colour you choose for your toned ground, opt for a tone that is mid-way between the lightest and darkest values in your painting.

Painting project: Teapot on a warm ground

For your first attempts at using a toned ground, try painting a simple subject on different colours of ground to see what difference it makes. You will probably find that the differences are quite subtle; nonetheless, the colour of the ground will have an impact on the overall mood and colour temperature of the painting.

In this exercise, we are working on a warm ground that complements the colour of the copper lustre teapot. The warm underpainting also serves to accentuate the coolness of the blues used to paint the background and table cloth. Versions of the same subject on a white ground and a blue ground, over the page, provide an interesting contrast.

You will need

- Acrylic paper
- HB pencil
- Acrylic paints: burnt sienna, cerulean blue, white, green, ultramarine blue, cadmium red, yellow, crimson
- Brushes: medium flat, small round, fine round or rigger

The set-up
Mix plenty of each colour shade, as you will often need to re-use it or use some of it as a base for new shades in later steps.

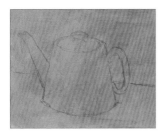

1 First, tone the support with burnt sienna acrylic paint. It doesn't matter if the coverage is slightly uneven. Leave to dry, then sketch your subject using an HB pencil.

2 Mix a very pale blue. Using a medium flat brush, block in the background above the table. The pale blue serves as a complementary colour to the burnt sienna ground – the contrast between the two gives the painting more impact.

3 Mix a bluish green from grass green, ultramarine blue and white and paint the cloth, darkening the mixture with more green for the shadow and the inner edge of the handle and a very dilute version for the cooler areas within the teapot, where the colour of the cloth is reflected.

④ Mix a pale, yellowish gold from cadmium red, yellow and white. Using a small round brush, put in the very brightest, irregularly shaped highlights, where light is hitting the teapot. These highlights should be applied as a very thin layer of paint; consequently, it is slightly modified by the burnt sienna ground.

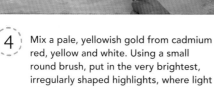

⑤ Mix a dark purple from crimson and ultramarine blue. Using a fine round or rigger brush, 'draw' a very fine line around the lid to imply the recess in which the lid sits. Use the same colour to paint the line of shadow under the pot. Add more green to the bluish green mixture from Step 3 and paint the reflections of the cloth at the base of the pot.

The finished painting

The burnt sienna ground gives an overall warmth and richness to the painting, as can be seen in the background, where hints of it remain visible through the thin blue-white paint.

It also serves as the deepest copper colour within the pot; the ground colour has not been painted over in these sections and this helps to unify the painting.

Hints of the toned ground remain visible through the thin blue-white mixture used to paint the background.

The burnt sienna ground is not completely covered over; here, it serves as the deepest copper colour within the pot.

White ground ▶

Here is the same scene on a white ground. A white ground tends to reflect a certain amount of light, even through a relatively opaque colour, which has the effect of making the overall key lighter. There is less interplay of colours within the metallic glaze of the pot and the highlights have been left as white, rather than painted on later.

Blue ground ▼

The version painted on a blue ground is cooler in mood. However, the blue ground is a good complementary colour for the coppery pot. Even small areas of blue underpainting, if allowed to show through, will have an effect on any adjacent colours.

Washes

Laying a wash – a thin layer of transparent colour – is common practice in acrylic painting, just as it is in watercolour painting. The idea is to apply fluid, thinned paint over areas that are too large to be covered by a single brushstroke. Washes are often used to form a base colour over which the image is then developed. As this tends to involve working over a large area, or even covering the whole of the support, always mix far more paint than you think you'll need: it's surprising how quickly you use it up, and if you run out, it can be very difficult to re-mix exactly the same shade. Before you apply the paint, prop your drawing board up on the easel at a slight angle, so that the paint can flow easily down the support.

There are various types of wash. A flat wash is a smooth, even layer of colour with no discernible differences in tone or visible brush marks. In a gradated wash, the colour shades from dark to light (or vice versa). A variegated wash, as the name suggests, consists of more than one colour. All washes are applied in a similar way, with the paint either merging wet into wet into another colour or spreading naturally over a damp support.

The main difference between watercolour and acrylic washes stems from the way in which the paints are manufactured. In watercolour paints, the pigments are bound with gum, which holds them together even when they are diluted with water to the point where the paint appears to be virtually colourless. In acrylic paints, the pigments are bound with an acrylic resin, which gives the paint body and substance; but if the paint is diluted too much, it begins to break down and any wash will look thin and lifeless. Because the paint has body, acrylic washes are easier to control than watercolour.

Laying a wash
This sequence demonstrates the technique of laying a flat wash. It is a good idea to add a little flow-improving medium, as this increases the flow of the paint; very thin paint tends to puddle rather than brush out evenly across a surface. For a gradated wash, add more water to the paint as you work down the paper. For a variegated wash, change to a different colour part way through.

 Using a large wash brush and working from left to right, lay a smooth stroke of colour across the support. Quickly re-load your brush with more paint. Pick up the pool of paint at the base of the first stroke with your brush and continue across the support, again working from left to right.

 Continue until you have covered the support. The paint should dry to a flat, even tone with no variation or visible brush marks.

Glazing

A glaze is a transparent layer of paint that is applied over a layer of paint. As with traditional watercolour, light passes through the transparent glaze and is reflected back by the support or any underpainting. Glazing is a form of optical mixing, as each glaze colour is separate from the next, with the mixing taking place within the eye. Each glaze needs to be dry before the next layer is applied, otherwise the colours will simply mix together as they would on the palette. Acrylic paints are ideal for glazing, as they dry very quickly.

Glazed colours reflect light more readily than opaque colours. This gives glazed works a richness and luminosity that can be lacking in paintings done using conventional mixing techniques.

Traditionally, the work begins with a tonal underpainting in monochrome over which the colours are carefully glazed. However, glazing techniques can also be used in conjunction with more opaque painting techniques. Glazes over opaque paint can liven up dull areas of colour, or make warm areas of colour appear cooler or cool areas warmer. This is particularly useful when painting portraits. A single colour glaze is often used over the entire finished picture to bring an overall harmony.

Physical colour mixing

Physically mixing cadmium yellow (below left) and dioxazine purple (below right) creates a dull brown (bottom left). When the colours are glazed one over the other, however, the integrity of both remains intact and the result is a brighter mix (bottom right).

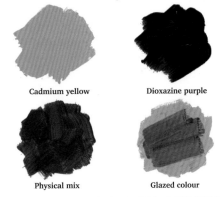

Cadmium yellow   Dioxazine purple

Physical mix   Glazed colour

Lightness or darkness of the glazed colour

When glazes are applied over a monochrome underpainting, the tones of the underpainting determine the lightness or darkness of the colours glazed on top.

Mediums for glazes

Add a gloss painting medium to acrylic paints for glazing, this not only thins the paint but also increases its transparency. Certain colours, which are by their nature more transparent, are more suitable for glazing techniques than others, but even opaque colour can be used.

Acrylic paint straight from the tube

Acrylic paint plus gloss medium

Wet into wet and blending

Allowing one wet paint colour to merge into another on the support is a very exciting way of painting and it can create some extremely atmospheric effects. The thinner the paint, the more the different colours will bleed into one another.

With acrylic paints mixed with lots of water, the technique is akin to that used in watercolour painting and the result depends on how wet the first colour is. If the first colour is still very wet, any subsequent colour will spread and blur, and the result will be soft and somewhat hazy – perfect for subjects such as skies or reflections in water. If the first colour or the support has dried a little, however, the paint will not spread so far – and the brush marks will have a harder edge.

Working wet into wet in this way will always be slightly unpredictable – but that is one of the charms of the technique and, with practice, you will get better at judging how far the paint is likely to spread.

Blending paint with a fan brush

Thick acrylic paints can be blended on the support, rather than in the palette, to create another colour. This technique is very effective where subtle gradations of colour are required.

1 Put the two colours down separately on the support. Here, we used cadmium red and cadmium yellow.

2 Using a fan brush, gently stroke one colour into the other so that the two blend together.

3 The two colours merge physically on the support to create a third colour – here, orange.

Blending wet acrylic paint with water

Another way to blend acrylic paint is to brush water onto an area of paint and then add your second colour. This is a great technique if one of your colours has already dried.

1. Put the first colour down on the support and leave it to dry. Brush clean water over part of the first colour.

2. Apply the second colour, painting up to the edge of the area that you wetted with clean water.

3. The second colour spreads into the wet area and mixes optically to create orange.

You will need
- Watercolour board
- 2B pencil
- Acrylic paints: alizarin crimson, cadmium yellow, phthalocyanine green, titanium white
- Brushes: large round, fine round

Painting project: Autumn leaves

In this exercise, red and green paints are allowed to merge into each other, blending together on the support to create subtle, soft-edged shifts from one colour to the next. Painting autumn leaves is a great way of practising the wet-into-wet technique, as you don't need to be terribly precise about where one colour ends and the next one begins.

The scene
These vine leaves are just beginning to turn from a glossy green to a rich red.

1. Using a 2B pencil, lightly sketch the outline of the leaves and the main veins.

2. Mix a warm, dilute red with a little yellow. Using a large, round brush, loosely brush this over the red parts of the leaves. You don't need to be precise, but try not to let paint to spill outside the leaves.

3 Mix a bright green. While the red paint is wet, brush the mixture over the brightest green leaves, allowing it to merge into the red. Darken the mixture, and paint the leaves on the bottom right of the image.

4 Mix a very dark green. Using a fine round brush, put in the most prominent veins. Hold the brush by the end of the handle, almost vertically to the support, and lightly touch it on to the support to get some variation in the line.

5 Mix a dark red and outline the edges of some of the redder leaves.

6 Using the dark green from Step 4, block in the spaces between the leaves. While the paint is still wet, mix some red into the green and drop it into the spaces, wet into wet. This adds a realistic colour variation to the shadows.

7 Continue working on the dark, shadowy spaces between the leaves. Defining these spaces will make the shapes of the leaves stand out more clearly from the background.

8 Now build up the leaves. Darken the red leaves with a very dilute mix of more red, adding some green in places to merge wet into wet. Add yellow to the bright green mixture from Step 3 and brush it on to the central leaf.

The finished painting

By working wet into wet, the artist has achieved some lovely, subtle colour shifts in the leaves, with pink merging into red, and red into varying shades of green. The joy of painting in this way is that you can allow the paint to flow of its own accord and do a lot of the work for you. The detail of the leaf veins was added when the first washes had almost dried, so these lines are crisper without overpowering the initial washes. By holding the brush near the end of the handle, however, the artist has been able to make lovely flowing lines like those used in Chinese brush painting or calligraphy. The result is an atmospheric, spontaneous-looking study.

9 Combine your basic red and green mixtures to make a very dark, almost black colour. Using a fine round brush held almost vertically, put in the very dark veins on the shaded red parts of the leaves. Mix a soft pink from titanium white and crimson and paint the pink leaf tips.

10 Add more of the yellowish green from step 8 to the central leaf. Use the dark green mixture from Step 4 to put in the veining on the leaf.

When one colour is applied on top of a colour that is almost dry, the second colour has a clearly discernible edge.

When two colours are allowed to merge wet into wet, the transition between the two is virtually imperceptible.

Scumbling

Scumbling is the technique that involves applying dry, semi-opaque paint loosely and roughly over a dry underlayer, leaving some of the underlayer visible to create optical colour mixes on the support. The technique also produces interesting surface textures in which the marks of the brush or other paint applicator may still be seen. The texture of the support plays an important part in scumbling techniques, which tend to be more successful on rough surfaces than on smooth. Having said that, however, subtle scumbling is useful for adding variation and relief to large areas of flat, uninteresting colour on smooth supports.

If an area looks too hot, you could scumble a cool colour over the top – and vice versa. Or you might choose to use the technique to paint an area of deep shadow, which is rarely if ever a uniform, flat colour. There are lots of subjects for which scumbling is appropriate. Masses of foliage seen from a distance, clouds racing across a stormy sky, torrents of water, worn stone or distressed wood: all consist of intermingling colours and can benefit from the fresh, spontaneous look that scumbling can achieve.

Whatever medium you are using, when applying a scumble you should always work loosely and freely.

Broad scumble
Here, a stiff mix of paint is scumbled over the dry, slightly textured paint applied previously.

Scumbling to add interest
An area of dry, flat colour can be made more interesting by scumbling a slightly different colour over it.

Transparent scumble
For a more transparent scumble and delicate optical colour mixes, add acrylic medium to the paint.

Heavily textured scumbling
For a more textured look, dot the paint on to the support straight from the tube.

Light scumbling with a rag
To allow more of the first layer to show through, dip a rag or absorbent kitchen paper into your chosen colour and lightly touch it on to the support, so that the paint adheres only to the peaks of the brushstrokes of the first layer.

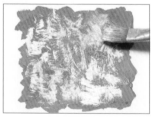

Light colour scumbled over dark
Use a stiff, dryish mix of paint and remove some of it from the brush prior to making the mark, in the same way as you would with drybrush techniques. This allows more of the first layer to show through.

Painting project: Distressed wood and metal

Scumbling is the perfect technique for painting weathered wood and metal, as it allows underlying colours to show through and creates interesting textures. Keep your paints fairly thick and dry, and apply the paint unevenly, so that the colour is not uniform.

You will need

- Cardboard primed with acrylic gesso
- HB pencil
- Acrylic paints: crimson, green, raw sienna, brown, green
- Matt acrylic medium
- Brushes: large round, small round, small flat

The scene
The artist came across this magnificent but rather scary-looking door knocker on a trip to Venice; small details such as this are often as evocative of the look of an entire building.

1 Using an HB pencil, sketch the scene. Although the subject is small in scale, the changes in tone from one plane to another need to be carefully rendered, so make sure you put in all the detail you need. Your pencil marks will be fully covered by the paint.

2 Mix a dark, almost black, green from crimson and green and add a few drops of matt acrylic medium. Using a large round brush, start painting the background.

3 Lighten the mixture for the top left of the painting, which is catching more of the light. Add some raw sienna to the mixture and brush it wet into wet into the background to get some variation in colour.

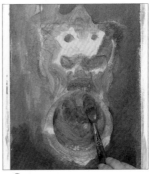

4 Mix a warm brown from raw sienna and crimson and dab it loosely over the darkest parts of the metal door knocker. This will serve as a warm base for subsequent applications of paint.

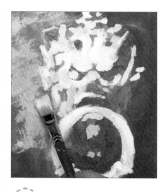

5   Mix an opaque, pale colour from titanium white and a little brown and green. Using a small round brush, brush it over the lightest areas, adding more green to the mixture for those areas that are slightly cooler in tone.

6   Continue to paint the door knocker, alternating between the warm and cool mixtures used in the previous step as necessary in order to build up the form. Leave to dry.

7   Mix an opaque white from titanium white and the cool green mixture. Using a medium flat brush, loosely scumble it over the wood of the door, allowing some of the underlying colour to remain visible, creating the effect of worn, distressed paintwork.

8   Continue to scumble over the door, adding more green for some parts and more light brown for others. The light in the scene is coming from the top left, which means that the bottom right is darker and more deeply shaded.

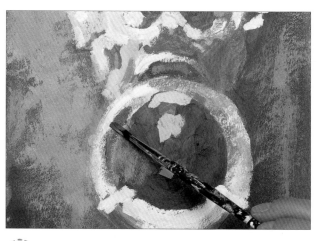

9   The scumbling on the door establishes the mid tones of the painting, which makes it easier to assess how dark the very shaded parts need to be. Mix a dark, brownish green. Using a small brush, put in the dark recesses on the face, adding more brown on the right-hand side. Scumble the same colour over the round knocker.

10 Build up the form by continuing to add shaded recesses on the face.

11 Refine the details, using opaque mixtures of all the colours on your palette. Use a small flat brush to sharpen the outline of the door knocker with dark greens and blue-green mixes.

Helpful Hint

The shape of the flat brush makes it easier to give objects a crisp, sharp outline.

The finished painting

This painting shows just how effective scumbling can be when painting worn and weathered surfaces. Although only a limited number of colours were used, the various layers of paint imply not only the way the wooden door has been bleached by years of exposure to the sun and rain, but also has rough textures. The use of warm and cool tones of the same colours creates a convincing sense of light and shade, even though the light source itself (the sun) is not visible. This helps to build up the form of the door knocker and make it look three-dimensional.

Rough scumbling adds texture to the image.

Here, the scumbling hints at the rustiness of the metal.

Removing paint

There are three main reasons for removing paint from your canvas or support: to get back to the original support, either so that you can reveal the underlying colour or so that you can paint over the area again and correct a mistake; to remove excess paint from an area that has become clogged with paint; and to work into paint to create textured marks.

Removing paint to get back to the original support

If the underlying colour is very strong, it's best to try and remove it so that it doesn't affect any subsequent glazes. The method that you select depends on the medium you are using and on whether the paint is wet or dry.

Remove wet acrylic paint

Dip a rag in water and wipe it through the paint.

Removing excess paint

When you're doing very heavy impasto work in acrylics, the canvas can become clogged with paint. If the effect is as you desire, then allow the paint to dry before applying more paint. If the effect is not what you intended, scrape off the paint and start again. Thick acrylic dries in hours, so it needs to be scraped off immediately. To remove excess paint, use one of the following methods.

Scraping off paint with a knife

Hold the edge of the knife perpendicular to the support, press down firmly, and drag the knife through the wet paint to remove any surplus. This leaves a flat area of colour, in which no brush marks can be seen.

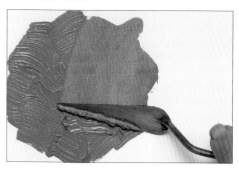

Tonking

An alternative method is a technique known as tonking – named after the British artist Henry Tonks (1862–1937).

1. Place a sheet of newspaper over the affected area and smooth it down with your hands.

2. Peel away the paper, removing any excess paint in the process. The result is more textured than using a knife.

Working into paint to create texture

Thick paint has a pleasing texture that comes from the marks left by the bristles of the brush. However, greater verisimilitude can often be achieved when replicating the textures present on whatever is being painted by working into the paint.

Sgraffito – wet paint

You can make textured marks in paint by scraping into the paint with the end of a brush. Alternatively, use a twig, the tip of a craft knife or the edge of a piece of cardboard.

Sandpaper – dried acrylic

To create texture on dried acrylic paint, lightly rub sandpaper or another abrasive material over the area. Do not rub so hard that you damage the support.

You will need

- Board primed with acrylic gesso
- B pencil
- Acrylic paint: cadmium yellow, white, red, dark green
- Retarding medium
- Small painting knife
- Newspaper
- Brushes: flat wash, medium flat, small flat

Two methods of lifting off paint are used in this exercise – tonking and scraping off paint with a knife. As acrylics dry quickly, it is a good idea to add a little retarding medium to your mixes as this gives you longer to work into the paint. Even so, it is best to work on relatively small areas – one melon at a time.

Painting project: Watermelons

The scene

The artist came across these watermelons on a market stall. Red and green are complementary colours and almost always work well together. The jagged lines of the cut melons counterbalance the rounded forms of the whole fruits.

1 Mix a pale yellow using cadmium yellow and white paint and with a flat wash brush, cover the board. Leave to dry. Using a B pencil, draw the outlines of the fruits. At this stage, you don't need to put in the jagged outlines of the cut melons: an indication of the overall shape, which you can use as a guideline, is sufficient.

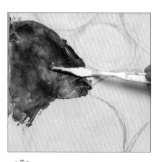

(2) Mix a dark green, adding a little retarding medium to the mixture to give yourself longer to work. Using a small painting knife, cover the first uncut watermelon with the mixture. The coverage does not have to be completely even, but try not to go outside the pencil lines.

(3) Tear off a piece of newspaper and scrunch it up into a long, thin strip. Press it firmly into the paint and lift it off to reveal the toned ground underneath. Note the lovely random textures and markings that this creates: it would be much more difficult to achieve this effect by painting on the lighter colour with a brush.

(4) Repeat Steps 2 and 3 until you have painted all the uncut watermelons, varying the dark greens by adding more cadmium yellow for some fruits and more olive green for others. Using a medium flat brush, fill in the spaces between the melons with a very dark green. The image immediately takes on more of a sense of depth.

(5) Mix a pinkish red (adding white paint to the red). Paint the red flesh of the cut melons, leaving a broad band of yellow around the edge. Place the knife tip in the centre of the melon, with the knife on its side, and scrape it clockwise, lifting off wedge-shaped areas of paint.

(6) Darken the pink mixture from the previous step by adding more red. Dip the side of the knife into the paint and press it on to the melons to create the jagged cuts in the surface. This helps to create shading and makes the surface of the melons look three-dimensional.

(7) Mix an opaque yellow. Using a medium flat brush, paint the zigzag-shaped cut edges of the melons.

9 Mix pale pink from red and white and then touch in the pale pinks in the melon flesh, taking the colour to the melon rim in places. Mix a pale off-white from titanium white and a little yellow and put in some thin highlight lines on the melon flesh.

8 Using the dark green mixture from Step 2 and a small flat brush, cut in around the edges of the melons to sharpen the shapes.

10 Mix together the dark green from Step 2 and the dark red from Step 6 to create a colour that is almost black. Paint the pips, using a small brush, and then scrape off the highlights on the pips using the end of your brush handle.

Helpful Hint

The dark green makes the watermelons stand out more.

The finished painting

This is a lively and energetic painting that uses the technique of lifting off paint to great effect to create interesting textures.

Colour has been lifted off to reveal the toned ground beneath, creating the pale stripes on the outside of the watermelons.

Scraping paint off with the side of a painting knife creates flatter, less textured areas of colour.

Drybrush

With the drybrush technique, the brush is loaded with the minimum amount of paint and then skimmed gently over a dry surface so that it catches on the raised tooth of the paper or canvas, leaving part of the support showing. It is important to splay out the bristles of the brush (or to use a fan brush) so that the individual bristle marks are evident on the support. Make sure your paint mix is not too wet.

Splaying out bristles
If you do not have a fan brush, you can splay out the bristles of an ordinary brush between your finger and thumb to create the same kind of marks.

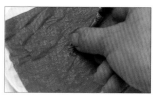

Loading the brush with paint
If you simply dip your brush into your palette, there is a risk that you will overload it. To avoid this, splay out the bristles and gently pull them over a paper towel soaked in paint.

Drybrush work over a large area
To cover a large area, dip the tip of a large bristle or household decorating brush in paint and gently drag it over the support, holding the brush at 90 degrees to the support.

Painting project: Seashells

You will need

- Cardboard primed with button polish
- HB pencil
- Acrylic paints: white, ultramarine blue, raw sienna, cadmium red, lemon yellow
- Absorbent kitchen paper
- Brushes: small flat, fine round

This simple still life consists of two large shells on a white background, simply lit from one side. One of the shells is placed upside down, enabling us to look inside it.

The delicate, linear markings and ridges on seashells such as these make them the perfect candidates for the drybrush technique.

1 Sketch the shells with an HB pencil. Paint the background in a dilute wash of white and ultramarine blue. Paint the shadows in a purplish grey mixed from ultramarine and raw sienna. Mix a warm-toned mix of white and raw sienna and a cool-toned mix of white and ultramarine. Alternating between them, begin painting the shells.

2 Mix a purplish colour from cadmium red and ultramarine blue. Load the paintbrush, dab off any excess paint on a piece of kitchen paper, and paint the dark colour on the inside of the left-hand shell. Add white to the mixture to make it more opaque and put in the dark markings on the other shell. Using a fine round brush and the warm-toned mixture from Step 1, drybrush the grooves on the shell.

3 Mix a dark purple from cadmium red and ultramarine blue and drybrush on the markings on the interior of the left-hand shell. Add a tiny amount of raw sienna to the cool-toned mixture from Step 1 and put in the slightly shaded areas of the right-hand shell, making sure your brushstrokes follow the direction of the grooves on the shells to reinforce the three-dimensional impression.

4 Mix a very pale yellow from lemon yellow and titanium white and paint the tops of the ridges on the right-hand shell. Continue putting in the dark patterning on the shells, using the drybrush technique all the time to create texture and imitate the rough, irregular markings on the shells.

5 Mix a mid-toned grey from titanium white, lemon yellow and raw sienna. Scumble the mixture over the background, carefully brushing around the shadows. Using the purple mixture from Step 3, reinforce the lines in the left-hand shell colours as before.

The finished painting
Drybrush work is the perfect way to paint these shells' small, spiny ridges. As the brushes are skimmed only lightly over the surface of the support, the technique also allows underlying colours to show through, conveying the mottled, irregular coloration of the shells very effectively.

Painting Project: Café scene

Congratulations – you're ready to try a complex scene painting! At first glance, this café and street scene looks extremely difficult and full of movement, with a complex play of light and shade across the whole scene. You could be forgiven for wondering how on earth you can capture such a wealth of detail in paint.

The trick, at least in the initial stages, is to forget about the detail and to concentrate instead on the overall impression. Look for blocks of colour and tone – and try to see the scene as a series of interconnecting shapes, rather than as individual elements. If you get too caught up in details such as a person's hair or the precise pattern on one of the café umbrellas, the chances are that your painting will become tight and laboured.

Remember, too, that the spaces between objects (which artists describe as 'negative' shapes) are as important in a painting as the objects themselves (the 'positive' shapes). Although the rational part of your brain may be telling you that a person or a solid object such as a table should take precedence over an apparently empty background, in painting terms the two are equally important: one helps to define the other.

The complex pattern of light and shade requires careful treatment, too. There are many shadows here, both in the open foreground and in the dark, narrow street in the background. Shadows are rarely, if ever, black; instead, they often contain colours that are complementary to the main subject. If buildings are a warm terracotta colour, for example, their shadows may contain a little complementary green.

You will need

- Board primed with acrylic gesso
- Willow charcoal
- Acrylic paint: lemon yellow, titanium white, grass green, ultramarine blue, brilliant purple, cadmium red
- Brushes: large round, medium flat, small round
- Absorbent paper towel

The scene

This is one type of subject in which painting from photographs really comes into its own. There is so much going on that you could do little more than put down the bare bones of the scene on the spot – but a quick reference photo or two will 'freeze' the action and provide you with plenty of information on which to base your image. Alternatively, you can make a preliminary sketch to also capture a moment.

1. Block in the darkest areas of the background buildings and the shadows on the pavement, using the side of a stick of willow charcoal, as this allows you to cover large areas quickly. Although the charcoal will be covered up by subsequent applications of paint, it allows you to establish the structure of the scene at the outset, and makes it easier for you to find your way around the complex mix of colours and tones.

2. To avoid dirtying your colours when you begin applying the paint, gently dust off any excess charcoal powder using a clean piece of paper towel. (Alternatively, you could use a spray fixative.)

3. Mix a warm orange. Using a large round brush, brush in the warm colours of background buildings. Paint the café umbrellas and awning in mixtures of cadmium red and titanium white, varying the proportions of the two colours to get the right tones. Putting in these strong tones in the early stages helps give the scene some structure. The order in which you apply them is not terribly important, but while you have got one colour on the palette try to use it everywhere that it occurs.

4. Loosely indicate the café tables in a cool-toned green (you can mix grass green with blue). Mix a very dilute green and paint the shadow areas in the foreground. (Note that this green is a cool complementary colour to the reds used on the awning and umbrellas.) Add red to the mixture and paint the very dark colours of the buildings in the background. This gives you the necessary darkness of tone without having to resort to using black, which often tends to look flat and lifeless. It also picks up on colours used elsewhere in the painting, creating one of many colour links that will ultimately help to hold the whole image together.

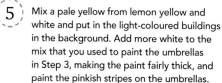

5 Mix a pale yellow from lemon yellow and white and put in the light-coloured buildings in the background. Add more white to the mix that you used to paint the umbrellas in Step 3, making the paint fairly thick, and paint the pinkish stripes on the umbrellas.

6 Using the dark mixture from Step 4, begin blocking in the figures sitting in the café. Do not try to put in substantial detail at this stage: simply look for the overall shapes. Look at the tilt of people's shoulders and heads and concentrate on getting these angles right. Brush more of the dilute green-and-white mixture over the street area, particularly at the point just beyond the café where the street narrows and is in deeper shade.

7 Block in the colours of the shirts of the café customers in the foreground (in tones of yellow, blue, and orange), making the colours darker in tone for the creases in the fabric, as this helps to reveal the form of the body and give more of a sense of light and shade.

8 Brush over the highlight areas with titanium white, applying the paint thickly in order to create some texture. Deepen the tones of the big foreground umbrella where necessary. Using the same dark mixtures as before, carefully brush around the figures sitting at the café tables; defining the negative shapes (the spaces between the figures) in this way helps to separate them from the background so that they stand out more clearly.

Assessment time

Using blues and reds, block in more of the shirt and trouser colours of the passers-by on the left. The main elements are now in place, and the rest of the painting will be a gradual process of refinement: although they may look like fairly abstract blocks of colour at this stage, the subjects will soon start to emerge more clearly. Training yourself to look for blocks of colour, rather than attempting to define every element, is a useful exercise.

The dark blocks laid down in Step 1 provide the structure for the image.

The people are painted as bold blocks of colour; detail can be added later once the basic shapes and colours are in place.

9 Pick out details using a small round brush. Paint the curved chair backs in green, and the hair of the café customers in various browns mixed from yellow and red. Go around the figures in a dark tone to help them stand out.

10 Define more of the negative spaces and colour on the clothes of the passers-by. Vertical strokes of green on the background buildings are a quick-and-easy way of implying the dark window recesses; the colour also provides a visual link with the green chairs in the foreground.

11 Because it is so bright, the eye is drawn to the paved foreground area, which looks empty. Using more of the green mixture from Step 6 and a medium flat brush, make broad horizontal strokes across to enhance the feeling of dappled light and create texture and interest.

12 Switch to a medium flat brush which will allow you to shape straight-edged elements, such as the eaves of the roofs (top right) and the table edges (bottom right), more precisely.

13 Using a pale, blue-grey mixture of titanium white and ultramarine blue, loosely indicate the lettering on the café awning. Continue adjusting tones across the whole scene: adding a pale, but opaque yellow to the background buildings reinforces the sense of light and shade, while the shadows on the ground can be made stronger with a bluish-purple mixture from brilliant purple.

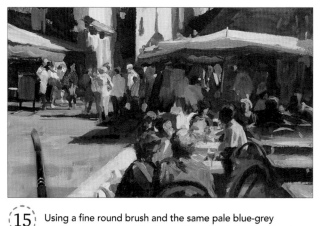

14 Using the flat brush again, block in rectangles of colour on the roofs to define their edges more clearly. The precise colours that you use are not too important: look for the relative lightness and darkness of different areas, as this is what will make the picture look three-dimensional.

15 Using a fine round brush and the same pale blue-grey mixture that you used for the café awning lettering, 'draw' in the vertical posts of the awning and the large foreground umbrellas. Adjust the tones if necessary, to reinforce the different planes of the image. If the bottom left corner is still too bright in relation to the rest of the painting, brush more of the bluey-green shadow mixture across it. Finally, look for any areas that catch the light, such as the edges of the foreground tables and chairs, and lightly touch in the highlights here with a pale mixture of grass green and titanium white.

The finished painting

This is a spontaneous-looking painting that belies its careful planning and the meticulous attention to capturing the effects of light and shade. The composition looks informal, like a snapshot of a moment 'frozen' in time; in fact, the large, virtually empty space on the left helps to balance the image, while the receding lines of the café tables lead the viewer's eye through the picture to the bustling street and buildings in the background.

Creating the right tonal balance is one of the keys to an image like this; resisting the temptation to put in too much detail, with the consequent risk of overworking the painting, is another.

Here, the artist has succeeded on both counts.

Deep shadows reveal the intensity of the sunlight. They are balanced by the large, brightly lit buildings in the background and help to bring the scene to life.

Although there is relatively little detail on the faces, by concentrating on the tilt of the heads and bodies the artist has conveyed a feeling of animation.

The artist has used some artistic licence in choosing the colours for the building in the background, but they complement and balance the foreground colours well.

Types of finish

Acrylic paints dry to leave a matt or slightly glossy surface. The finish depends entirely on the brand being used. Gloss or matt mediums can be added to leave the surface with the desired finish. Gloss and matt mediums can also be mixed together to give the dry paint varying degrees of sheen. The choice is a personal one. As a general rule, colours on a gloss surface tend to look brighter. It is also preferable to use gloss mediums when glazing colours.

Gloss and matt mediums

It is impossible to tell simply by looking at it whether a medium will give a matt or a gloss finish. Both gloss (left) and matt (right) mediums are relatively thin white liquids that dry clear if applied to a support without being mixed with paint.

Gloss Medium

Matt Medium

The effect of gloss medium

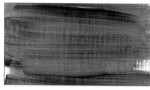

Adding gloss medium to the paint increases its transparency. This allows you to build up several thin glazes relatively quickly, leaving the dry paint with a slight gloss sheen. Gloss medium also enhances the depth of colour, improves adhesion to the support and increases the flexibility of the paint. It can be used as an adhesive for collage work. Some manufacturers also advise using gloss medium as a varnish.

The effect of matt medium

Matt medium also increases transparency and can be used to make matt glazes. Matt medium has good adhesive properties. It can be thinned with water and used to size canvas, or diluted 50:50 with water and used as a fixative for drawings. Matt mediums are not generally used as varnish, as they can deaden colour and look slightly cloudy.

Continuing your acrylic journey

You now have the basic skills that you need to practise acrylic painting! Of course, this is just the start of your artistic journey; there are always more techniques to learn, more styles to try and you can always hone your techniques. One brilliant way to challenge yourself and find inspiration is to do plein air painting – that is painting outdoors. Let the natural light and surroundings inspire you and learn to capture that particular moment in time.